THAT THIS

Also Available by Susan Howe from New Directions

The Europe of Trusts
Frame Structures: Early Poems 1974–1979
The Midnight
My Emily Dickinson
The Nonconformist's Memorial
Pierce-Arrow
Souls of the Labadie Tract

THAT THIS

SUSAN HOWE

A NEW DIRECTIONS BOOK

Some of these poems are previously published: "That This" originally appeared in *The Nation*. "Frolic Architecture" was published in a limited edition by Grenfell Press in 2010 with photograms by James Welling. A portion of "The Disappearance Approach" was in the *Chicago Review* as part of "Choir answers to Choir." Much of the material in "Frolic Architecture" is collaged from the "private writings" of Hannah Edwards Wetmore, copied by her daughter Lucy Wetmore Whittelsey, now among the Jonathan Edwards papers at the Beinecke Library. In places I relied on Kenneth Minkema's transcription.

AUTHOR'S NOTE: Thanks are due to Megan Mangum of Words That Work.

Cover and interior design by Leslie Miller, The Grenfell Press
Manufactured in the United States of America
New Directions Books are printed on acid-free paper.
First published as New Directions Paperbook 1189 in 2010
Published simultaneously in Canada by Penguin Canada Books, Ltd.

Library of Congress Cataloging-in-Publication Data
Howe, Susan, 1937–
That this / Susan Howe.
p. cm.
ISBN 978-0-8112-1918-1 (pbk. : alk. paper)
I. Title.
PS3558.O893T43 2010
811'.54—dc22

2010041791

10 9 8 7 6 5 4 3 2

New Directions Books are published for James Laughlin
by New Directions Publishing Corporation
80 Eighth Avenue, New York 10011

CONTENTS

The Disappearance Approach 11

Frolic Architecture 39

That This 99

[untitled] 109

THE DISAPPEARANCE APPROACH

In memory of Peter H. Hare (1935–2008)

It was too quiet on the morning of January 3rd when I got up at eight after a good night's sleep. Too quiet. I showered, dressed, then came downstairs and put some water on the boil for instant oatmeal. Peter always woke up very early, he would have been at work in his study, but there was no sign of his having breakfasted. I looked out the window and saw *The New York Times* still on the driveway in its bright blue plastic wrapper. Had he gone for a walk? I checked to see if his slippers were on the floor by the window seat where he usually left them when he went out. They weren't there. Why? The water was boiling, I poured it over the cereal, stirred it, then stopped. The house was so still. I called his name. No answer. Was he sick or had he overslept? I remember thinking I shouldn't eat until I was sure he was all right. We had a running joke that at seventy anything might happen so if one of us didn't appear in the morning by nine, the other should check. I called his name again. Again, no answer. Maybe he didn't hear me because he was taking a shower. I went into his room. He was lying in bed with his eyes closed. I knew when I saw him with the CPAP mask over his mouth and nose and heard the whooshing sound of air blowing air that he wasn't asleep. No.

Starting from nothing with nothing when everything else has been said

—

"O My Very Dear Child. What shall I say? A holy and good God has covered us with a dark cloud." On April 3, 1758, Sarah Edwards wrote this in a letter to her daughter Esther Edwards

Burr when she heard of Jonathan's sudden death in Princeton. For Sarah all works of God are a kind of language or voice to instruct us in things pertaining to calling and confusion. I love to read her husband's analogies, metaphors, and similes.

For Jonathan and Sarah all rivers run into the sea yet the sea is not full, so in general there is always progress as in the revolution of a wheel and each soul comes upon the call of God in his word. I read words but don't hear God in them.

—

On the morning of January 2nd, we took the train into Manhattan to be part of my son's noon wedding at City Hall. That afternoon we couldn't find seats together on the crowded peak hour Metro North from Grand Central so we sat apart. It was dark when we arrived at New Haven and crossed the track for the Shoreline connection to Guilford. When we got off I walked quickly across the parking lot to the car. He followed more slowly. I wondered why, but it was so cold I didn't bother to look back. At home we cooked up some vegetables and pasta. After dinner he said he was tired and would go straight to bed.

—

"Oh that we may kiss the rod, and lay our hands on our mouths! The Lord has done it. He has made me adore his goodness, that we had him so long. But my God lives; and he has my heart....

We are all given to God: and there I am, and love to be." I admire the way thought contradicts feeling in Sarah's furiously calm letter.

We can't be limited to just this anxious life.

—

Somewhere I read that relations between sounds and objects, feelings and thoughts, develop by association; language attaches to and envelopes its referent without destroying or changing it—the way a cobweb catches a fly.

—

Now—putting bits of memory together, trying to pick out the good while doing away with the bad—I'm left with one overwhelming impression—the unpresentable violence of a negative double.

—

He was lying with his head on his arm, the way I had often seen him lie asleep. I thought of Steerforth's drowned body in *David Copperfield*, also the brutality of sending young children away to boarding school in order to forge important ties for future life. Though Steerforth is a sadistic character his perfect name forms a second skin. Something has to remain to rest a soul against stone.

—

The CPAP mask was over his face because he had sleep apnea, a disorder characterized by pauses in breathing during sleep. When the mask is plugged in and running, pressure greater than the surrounding atmosphere is enough to keep the upper airways from becoming narrowed or blocked. If he felt anything unusual, surely he would have tried to remove the cumbersome thing. It was still running in place and fogged up.

Land of darkness or darkness itself you shadow mouth.

—

A cold clear day. I'm at the computer in his study deleting spam, saving folders and e-mails for the *Transactions of the C. S. Peirce Society: A Quarterly Journal in American Philosophy*, a magazine he co-edited for many years. I scroll to mail dated 1/2/08. There's a note from a colleague concerning the annual meeting of the eastern division of the American Philosophical Association in Baltimore they attended the week before. "We all need quiet time now after the busy fall—Shannon."

That night or was it early morning, Peter took eternal wordlessness into himself.

—

Some paperwhites he loved to plant and bring to flower are thriving in our living room. Paperwhites are in the daffodil family so have their sweet spring scent. Blooming in winter they represent happiness that costs next to nothing simply by receiving the sun's brightness, repose and harmony. On the computer screen I find a short essay he was writing on poetry and philosophy but never showed me. There's a letter to his first wife's brother, signed, "Peter and Sukey." I wish we were Hansel and Gretel with pebbles as a hedge against the day before and the day after.

Once you admit that time past is actually infinite, being a child gradually fades out.

—

Looking over autobiographical fragments he wrote during the years following his first wife's death every one of them begins with his shock at her absence. If you looked through my papers until now, you would find a former dead husband at the center. We had almost stopped needing to summon the others—not quite. Not if you rely on written traces.

Fallible and faithful—what makes loyalty so righteous in measurable space? Forever following a river to the ramparts where they form a single plume in the center we are together in our awareness of the great past founded by Daphne and David. Everything appears in a deliberately constructed manner as if the setting of our story was always architectural.

—

"At any rate." Time and again you repeated this phrase. Often you had a hard time touching down in conversation—waving your arms and going off on tangents before coming the long way round to where you started. "Bang for the buck." I was impatient with your verbal tics. "All squared away." Now I would turn to listen with elation.

—

Today I found I had forgotten to pay the land tax due the first of January so there's an added punishment fee of one hundred and twenty-six dollars. If only we could return to December so I could let you know I needed you because I know you needed to be needed

as vast a need as at this moment.

—

"You can save money—it's to save you."

The imposing front door of Peter's large house in the Central Park section of Buffalo was simple mahogany with a polished brass knocker at its center. Shortly after we met he said why don't you just leave your rented place and come live with me here. In a primogenial sense it was the first wife's territory. I didn't share her taste. Nevertheless, old family oil portraits, various objects from the China Trade, engravings of genteel nineteenth-century Episcopalian ministers, and over the dining room table a painting of "The US Squadron Commanded by Comd. S. Rodgers sailing from Port Mahon. Respectfully dedicated to M. C. Perry Esq. of the U.S.N. by his most obt. Servant S. Cabrolla, Gibralta, 10 May 1826" in its solid wood frame beckoned me into an environment where ancestors figured as tender grass springing out of the earth. There they were, saying "Susan, child of our history, come home, come on in."

—

Maybe there is some not yet understood return to people we have loved and lost. I need to imagine the possibility even if I don't believe it.

—

Now if I think about that door, I remember my mother reading Hans Andersen's "The Little Match Girl" aloud when we lived in Buffalo during the months after Pearl Harbor was bombed. The match girl is so poor she is anonymous. Huddled in the snow outside some houses on New Year's Eve she strikes one last wick to warm her fingers. Light flares, and the wall of a building is suddenly transparent as scrim. She sees a table with roast goose, pears, all sorts of food on beautiful china; the happiness and light inside surrounds her.

What treasures of knowledge we cluster around. Fear—reunited with other pre-communicable penumbral associations. God is an epigraph inscribed on memory. Blown back among ghosts—our abstract Parent restores order with covering rituals.

—

Inside the Buffalo house the room I loved most was the study upstairs. He rarely used it then except as storage space for his many books. A large dilapidated desk that his father, a modernist architect, designed and constructed during the 1930s, was littered with old syllabi, letters and journals. A worn wall-to-wall carpet hushed the place and I had the same intense impression of the past pressing heavily on the present I often feel when I'm alone with books and papers. "I'll go to him—I'll find him," I thought, while rifling through old photograph albums. You could say I was intruding on another family's need to keep close once and for all—but relic rows of figures, once aware of the fact of being photographed, now enclosed in a paper world of their own, seemed to offer reluctant consent to being viewed face-to-face, in combined string voice.

—

I've been reading some of W. H. Auden's *The Sea and the Mirror*. One beautiful sentence about the way we all reach and reach but never touch.

A skinny covering overspreads our bones and our arms are thin wings.

—

In an early morning half-waking dream you were lying on the bed beside me in a dark suit. I recently touched your black jacket, the one you loved we bought together on sale two years ago in Barney's. We were thinking about getting another this month because you had worn the original to pieces—it's in the closet now, an object for storage beside your ashes. Maybe the jacket was in my mind as distant dream knowledge of the way one figure can substitute for another with a cord attached so what is false gives life to what is fair. I thought you were really you until I woke up back in myself.

—

History intersects with unanswered questions while life possesses us, so we never realize to the full one loyal one—only an elegiac ideal. I remember needing to take off and turn off the fogged-up plastic sleep apnea mask.

Your head was heavy as marble against the liberty of life.

—

The paperwhites are blooming wonderfully. They resemble February in its thin clarity. Spare white blooms against watery green leaves and white and off-white pebbles around each ochre half-exposed bulb: the blue hyacinth I bought at Stop & Shop is also flowering. Alone with the tremendous silence of your absence, I want to fill this room between our workspaces with flowers because light flows through them—their scent is breath or spirit of life against my dread of being alone—of being cheated by people—today the electrician—next week Greco and Haynes for the well water filter.

—

Sometimes, introducing himself to people, he enjoyed adding, "Peter Hare as in Peter Rabbit."

Esther (1695–1766)
Elizabeth (1697–1733)
Anne (1699–1790)
Mary (1701–1776)
Jonathan (1703–1758)
Eunice (1705–1788)
Abigail (1707–1764)
Jerusha (1710–1729)
Hannah (1713–1773)
Lucy (1715–1736)
Martha (1718–1794)

If your names are only written and no "originals" exist, do you have a real existence for us? What happens to names when time stops?

Answer: Nothing happens: There is no when.

—

Jonathan Edwards was the only son among ten unusually tall sisters their minister father jokingly referred to as his "sixty feet of daughters." Esther Stoddard Edwards, also known for her height, taught her eleven children and others in Northampton in a school that consisted of a downstairs room in their farmhouse. Later they received the same education Timothy provided to local boys in his parish in East Windsor, Connecticut. The girls were tutored along with their brother (in some cases they tutored him) in theology, philosophy, Latin, Greek, Hebrew, history, grammar and mathematics. All except Mary were sent to finishing school in Boston. All married late for that period. Mary remained single in order to care for her parents and grandparents. The Beinecke Library in New Haven owns a vast collection of Edwards family papers. It contains letters, diaries, notebooks, essays, and more than twelve hundred sermons; but apart from a journal kept by Esther Edwards Burr (Jonathan and Sarah's eldest daughter) after her marriage, and a few letters to and from the sisters, daughters, and Sarah, all that remains of this 18th-century family's impressive tradition of female learning are a bedsheet Esther Stoddard Edwards probably spun and embroidered herself, Sarah's wedding dress fragment, and several pages from Hannah Edwards Wetmore's private writings—along with posthumous excerpts collected and transcribed with commentary by her daughter Lucy Wetmore Whittlesey.

The Connecticut Historical Society in Hartford owns a fragment of Mary Edwards' crewel embroidery, and a pair of silk shoes "worked by Miss Hannah Edwards daughter of the Rev. Timothy Edwards, wife of Seth Wetmore, Esq. of Middletown."

Only tossing color coins into a well of language, while faces of magic contained in little stories outside the purview of philosophy scramble to help each other—quid pro quo.

—

The folio-size double leaves Jonathan, Sarah, and his ten tall sisters wrote on were often homemade: hand-stitched from linen rags salvaged by women from worn out clothing. Grassroots out-of-tune steps and branches, quotations of psalms, dissonant scripture clusters, are pressed between coarse cardboard covers with frayed edges. The rag paper color has grown deeper and richer in some. One in particular, with a jacket he constructed from old newspapers then tied together at the center with string, looks like a paper model for a canoe. The minister or possibly some later scholar has christened his antique paper vessel "The Doctrine of [the] Justice and Grace of God, Explained and Defended, and the Contrary Errors that Have of Late Prevailed, Confuted . . ."

—

Even if ideas don't exist without the mind, there may be copies or resemblances. I never clearly understood what "academic" meant in relation to philosophy's defining essence, but Peter always used the term when speaking of the structure of his intellectual life. Perhaps he was suddenly indifferent to this self-willed world of cultural symbols, intellectual-historical records, competing research topics, future career trajectories—making a splash with books.

—

There was a curtness to the way he left. After Mark and Frances were married, our wedding party lunched together at the Odeon in Tribeca. I remember he was unusually quiet as if he had a prevision of his own unmaking and felt the cinders in our happy chatter.

—

It's snowing heavily and due to continue. Trapped in the house by weather I have been going over his photographs. None of us (apart from his colleagues at Buffalo) encouraged the hobby, certainly not this family of artists. In October he flew to Romania for an international conference on pragmatism, society, and politics at the Constantin Brancusi University in Targu-Jiu, where he was giving a paper. While there, every minute he could spare from meetings and panels, he photographed houses, gardens, sculptures, and churches until his Hasselblad camera was crushed when a car backed over it in a parking lot. This could have been an omen. The blood clot that later killed him probably formed in his leg during the long flights over and back. What if our interior innermost mortal happiness is all we see without ever being able to show? I wonder what to do now with these truancies from professional philosophy.

—

C.O. Milford Pa. 1904.
The way bleak north
presents itself here
as Heraclitean error
driving and driving
thought and austerity
nearer to lyricism
Often as black ice

I wrote this poem on a winter day in 1998 when my mother was still alive, and I hadn't met Peter. I had been reading Xerox copies of the last journal pages from the microform edition of the manuscripts of Charles Sanders Peirce. If you take immediate environment into account, during the winter of 1904 things were threadbare for the putative father of Pragmatism. No peace in projects—no firewood for warmth—a few crotchety word lists used as ornaments or phantom limbs—I remember the way the lines came to me suddenly, after reading the journal, and how quiet it seemed inside the room with soft snow falling outside.

Nietzsche says that for Heraclitus all contradictions run into harmony, even if they are invisible to the human eye. Lyric is transparent—as hard to see as black or glare ice. The paved roadway underneath is our search for aesthetic truth. Poetry, false in the tricks of its music, draws harmony from necessity and random play. In this aggressive age of science, sound-colored secrets, unperceivable in themselves, can act as proof against our fear of emptiness.

Sorrows have been passed and unknown continents approached.

—

> "**au'top•sy**, n. [Gr. αυτοψια; from αυτος, self, and όψις, sight.] Personal observation or examination; ocular view. '*Autopsy* convinceth us that it hath this use.' *Ray*."

The final seven-page Autopsy Report from the Department of Pathology arrived in the mail today.

Extracts:

CAUSE OF DEATH in caps. EMBOLIC OBSTRUCTION OF THE RIGHT VENTRICULAR OUTFLOW TRACT.

Pathologist, Demetrios Braddock, M.D.

—Report Electronically Signed Out.—

"Eyes: The body is received with the eyes previously removed."

—

Dear Dr. Braddock:

If you die in your sleep do you know you are dead? Your clinically precise word order is a failure of dream-work. It gives an effect of harmless vacancy. Why this violent tearing away?

Sincerely,

—

An old friend came for the day and brought me the exhibition catalogue for *Poussin and Nature: Arcadian Visions*. A week later I went in to see the show at the Metropolitan. After the first visit I returned for solace and pardon, several times.

The actors I encounter in Poussin's world have names ingrafted from myth and scripture. At the dawn of thought river gods are keeping watch. Venus offers herself to the gaze of shepherds. Is she sleeping or pretending? Saint Jerome is kneeling in prayer by a cross. Some people follow nature's movement others are blind to divine and supernatural light. Eurydice mortally wounded by a viper, sees her fate. No one else does. Orpheus obliviously strums his lyre for the wedding guests who have placed themselves in position for the familiar song; everything in proportion.

In 2000 the Getty Museum hung two landscape paintings by Nicolas Poussin—*Landscape with a Man Killed by a Snake*, then on loan from the National Gallery in London, and their own *Landscape with a Calm*, alone together in one small exhibition room. T. J. Clark, who was there on a Getty Fellowship, decided to describe his experience of viewing them each day at different hours. In *The Sight of Death: An Experiment in Art Writing* he describes his process as "writing pictures to death, which is what most writing on art inevitably ends up doing, to have always embedded in the *form* of the narrative the (false) suggestion that once upon a time, back there and in the present, at the end and the beginning, the picture lived everlastingly here and now.

Among many other things *Landscape with a Snake* . . . puts that fiction of visibility to the test." Some art historians believe Poussin conceived *Landscape with Orpheus and Eurydice* as a pendent to *Snake*.

For Jonathan Edwards, snakes represent the venomous nature of the speech of wicked men. Tongues are weapons. "They have sharpened their tongue like a serpent."

—

Blind Orion Searching for the Rising Sun.

I'm entering this open prose area in order to assuage the early loss of an early father in an earlier grandfather scion childself. Names are signs for ideas settled in the mind. Poussin and Edwards are supposed to exist until there is no such thing. No steady name.

—

In Ovid's *Metamorphoses* the fruit of the mulberry tree is forever turned black by the red blood of Pyramus. This is how Poussin introduces the narrative of love turning to misfortune into a composition he originally meant to present as merely a *Landscape with a Storm*. "All the figures one sees there are playing their roles according to the weather; some are fleeing through the dust, in the direction of the wind that is driving them along . . . others, on the contrary, are going against the wind, walking with difficulty, covering their eyes with their hands. . . . In the foreground of the painting, one sees Pyramus lying dead on the ground, and near him Thisbe, who has succumbed to grief." Clark says that in *Landscape with Pyramus and Thisbe*—everything ominous in *Snake*—size, scale of the figures in relation to the whole, use of light, intensity of dumb show, framing and shaping—runs over the edge into chaos.

By 1650 Poussin's hands were shaking so badly he was painting through the tremors; in spite of his affliction the surface of the lake at the center of *Pyramus* is smooth as glass.

This still eye reflects a neutral "you" that is me; and yet secret. Who can hold such mirroring cheap? It's a vital aspect of marriage and deep friendship.

—

Jean Redpath is singing "The Raggle Taggle Gypsies" on my iPod. Her voice brings my mother into the room with poems and ballads we read together during the Second World War when my father was away in Europe. She preferred ones, like Yeats' "The Stolen Child" or Arnold's "The Forsaken Merman," where people disappear into never-answered questions. Listening now, it's as if a gate opens through mirror-uttering to an unknowable imagining self in heartbeat range.

When we listen to music we are also listening to pauses called "rests." "Rests" could be wishes that haven't yet betrayed themselves and can only be transferred evocatively.

I wonder at vocalism's ability to rephrase or reenact meaning and goodness even without the wished-for love. Can a trace become the thing it traces, secure as ever, real as ever—a chosen set of echo-fragments? The sound of Peter's voice communicated something apart from the words he was saying. Listening —I experienced early memories or mental images in distant counterpoint.

—

Both parents died young. He often said that after his first wife's early death in 1995 he felt sure he wouldn't live into his seventies. As if the car, with his mother, father, and Daphne inside, was waiting at the door.

—

An official in the faux-Gothic-gatehouse at the Delaware Avenue entrance to Buffalo's Forest Lawn Cemetery, where urns containing "cremains" are officially approved and money for the internment changes hands, politely insisted he knew Mr. Hare had a wife, but I wasn't her.

"We're together, we're together," I told myself. All I lack is your personal name on a tilted stone.

—

GEN MSS 151, Box 24, Folder 1379. Hannah Edwards, Diary Fragment/ca. 1739

"My Dear Children,

What shall I leave to you or what shall I say to you. Fain would I do something while I live that may contribute to your real benefit and advantage—our lives are all exceeding brittle and uncertain ..."

—

The Beinecke Rare Book and Manuscript Library, one of the largest buildings in the world devoted entirely to rare books and manuscripts, was constructed from Vermont marble and granite, bronze and glass, during the early 1960s. The Library's digital photography studio is located in a windowless room downstairs. Here objects to be copied according to the state-of-the-art North Light HID Copy Light system are prepared for reproduction. Each light is packed with 900 watts of ceramic discharge lamps and requires a typical 15-ampere, 120-volt outlet. The lamps are doubly fan-cooled, with one chamber for the hot (lamp) side and one fan for the electronic side. A diffusion screen spreads light evenly onto the copyboard while protecting the art object or manuscript from heat. This can be replaced with white Plexiglas for three-dimensional art work. Black curtains surrounding the copy table protect the photographer's vision and at the same time prevent light intensity from bleeding. One or two stuffed oblong cloth containers, known in the trade as snakes, hold the volume open. Facing pages are held down flat with transparent plastic strips.

"... & when I was out of my head, & thought myself sick & lost, or at a River Side & and among strangers that would not direct me home."

That's Hannah Edwards remembering her delirium during an illness in 1736. Under the fan-cooled copy lights, she speaks to herself of the loneliness of being Narcissus.

—

On the Shoreline Express I like to sit on the side where between Stony Creek and Guilford I can see my neighbor's house, and in winter a little further up the road catch a split-second glimpse of ours through the window as the train passes. I suppose I'm trying to capture a moment before mirror vision—because when you view objects that lie in front of your eyes as well as others in the distance behind, what you see in the mirror has already been interpreted—so far as you can tell.

More and more I have the sense of being present at a point of absence where crossing centuries may prove to be like crossing languages. Soundwaves. It's the difference between one stillness and another stillness. Even the "invisible" scotch tape I recently used when composing "Frolic Architecture" leaves traces on paper when I run each original sheet through the Canon copier.

—

"Love in a Universe of Chance"

Yesterday afternoon while out walking on Old Quarry Road I stopped by a small pond. There at the edge of the water among the reeds was a single swan. "Stately, still, remote, assured, majestically indifferent and composed." Swans usually have mates but this one was solitary in the dying light. William Gass speaks about the impossibility of ever perfectly translating Hölderlin's image of the birds dipping their heads "ins *heilignüchterne* Wasser" because the religious undertones in the single German word carry echoes of holy water and grace and when you break the syllables apart for English meaning, what is hallowed inside perishes.

—

Outside the field of empirically possible knowledge is there a property of blueness in itself that continues to exist when everything else is sold away? I keep going back in my mind to the tiny square remnant of Sarah Pierrepont's wedding dress. This love relic has lasted over two hundred years in the form of a Prussian blue scrap. It says nothing at all to an outsider who can look at it without being seen. Could it be an illusory correlation that causes my brain to repetitively connect this single swatch with the oblong royal blue plastic throwaway sheath—protecting the early edition of *The New York Times* as it lay on our driveway on the morning of January 3rd, and again with the bright cyan book jacket on the complimentary copy of *Richard Rorty: The Making of an American Philosopher* that arrived for Peter in the mail a month later?

—

"Safe, through this wall your loving words used to pass in tiny whispers."

Pyramus picks up Thisbe's cloak and carries it to the mulberry trysting-tree. The cerulean toga streaming across the running man's body and the blue fragment of Sarah's wedding dress coexist in limit and in freedom where all things are transacted and spoken, even the fable of Orpheus being permitted to redeem his wife from hell, though losing her afterwards by looking back, then through grief dwelling in deserts. I don't pretend to be saying God has promised any new grace concerning our scheme being brought to pass via parables of lost sheep. No, not the least shadow association even in the realm of wishes. Art is a mystery; artifice its form. Hannah has taken off her embroidered shoes.

She is dipping her bare feet in varieties of light.

—

I can't remember if there was snow on the ground but I do remember the cold. If winter landscape meets the being of the subject of the soul now and before, and conveys what is yours to join the finished pastoral invention of others that is rationalism's secret.

—

Returning home, after only a day or two away, I often have the sense of intruding on infinite and finite local evocations and wonder how things are, in relation to how they appear. This sixth sense of another reality even in simplest objects is what poets set out to show but cannot once and for all.

If there is an afterlife, then we still might: if not, not.

—

Midas begged Bacchus to relieve him of his dangerous talent. He has gone down to the source of the Pactolus River and kneels in profile, finally cleansed of gold. He is tired tired. In Poussin's small Ajaccio composition, yellow brushstrokes on leaves tipped by the setting sun indicate evening's reflective melancholy. There will always be people struggling for worldly power—

Do we communicate in mirror languages, through some inherent sense of form, in every respect but touch? Do we ever know each other; know who we really are? Midas, King Midas —is the secret we take away with us—touch

—

Storytellers in the expanding middle class eager for professional careers move across sites of struggle in "battleground" fields. We are our soul but we haven't yet got the dead of it. You steal on me you step in close to ease with soft promise your limit and absolute absence.

—

"Our ling'ring Parents—" At the end of Milton's poem "They looking back, all th'Eastern side beheld / Of Paradise, so late their happy seat." Now they mean to go to the end of the world —here—

"where the body goes, ceases to be, comes to nothing—"

—

It could have been the instant of balance between silence, seeing, and saying; the moment before speech. Peirce would call this moment, secondness. Peter was returning to the common course of things—our world of signs

FROLIC ARCHITECTURE

Into the beautiful meteor of the snow.

Emerson

That this book is a history of

a shadow that is a shadow of

me mystically one in another

Another another to subserve

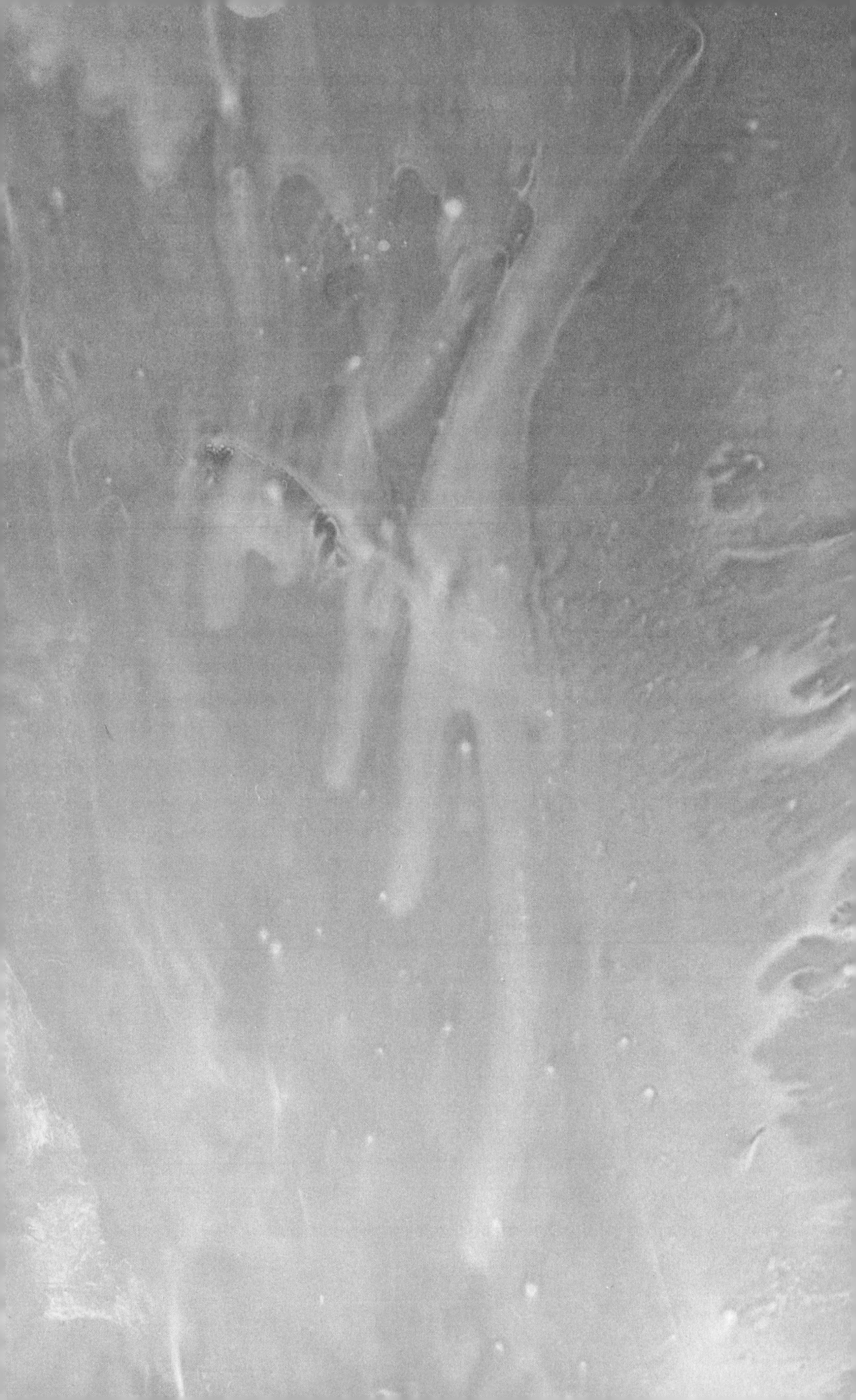

in one. No sun
ıor did the waxin
ɔt yet did the ear
n the circumamb
ed her arms alon
l, though there v
e could tread th
air was dark. N
; all objects w
ld things strov

ıent
n the
ler h
own
ɔcean
e lan
nd aı
sea ;
ned tı

lacun
lioses "Tri
verter etc.
in labored after an awake
Author,
of Liberty to go
eponderate why blame
ence a
akening sen

lacu "Trt
linses xerter etc.
in labored after an awakening

was leanin

ing body my body slipping

d down full toward its own

secret	sermon	rough
a myst	sermon	of grac
n and i	sermon	sent t

Oh! That I
be at rest
more sure
these allu
shaddowe
long shall
finding no
but find a
bewildered,
weary of my
That is first

Then
was
ever
for they
ever
had

had the wings of a dove tha
, but whether could , I fly,Oh
& abiding PORTION and no
ring, deceiving, enjoyment
s, where shall I find Real
I wander from mountain
ne---Oh that I could fin
rest for the sole of m
and weary myself t

ıe h

in profile, finally cl nt

ugh leaves in lower left ha

hing for the pieces of paper

pattern loth a e

in the edges around
their prison
QU'APRES CE
PREDICATEUR
ON LE PEUT AP bodies th
hand of Lucy Wetmore Whittelsey
Midae ; nec Delius aures
with comm
Box 24 Folder 1377.
t life a dark

what s
nters
onne.
nt R
he
ing
yir
d
ro

.. We need all three! Amaz ng. He

is . door swinging open and shut carpet

glass in.1208 EF G 3 of 3 folders. e out

ernist hush brittle tent cove

is all glas grace th little Fold ink has e last w the finer parch- again

cover ask Har re

out one out the last word on the thin fan out there

ust to make the final book a h paper in- that whe

pened but one word Hark! I cant ma side at s

walking just below my father's orchard (after I ha

walking just below my father's orchard (after I ha
eligion and the concerns of my soul my busines

religion and the concerns of my soul my busine
prayed for an labored after an awakening sense o

ter I had taked (after I had taken up many res-
concerns of my business, an: after I had set
to it, and praying sense of m, miserable con-
my miserablght with a great deal of concern
sensible, I thde and negligent, notwithstand-
ing so old in aning over the :outh fence and
notwithstandto be sensible :han now what
made me cast in my mind w: ether I had not
ural. But I considered I was ve y unable to jud
I was leaning in one chain ci thought, I saw
manner, that an image of it on my mind as
what should be, but I attempted to read, but
out one chain intercepting a id covering the
I had as lively asible, and did not seem to be
had seen it wiabruptly and :o strong that it
I attempted to n to look upo it as supernat-
by a piece of sower of imagination, and that

aper band/n.d. Folder 137

e kept up I always hoped for
; I seemed to be set at gre
concern with it, it then ap
l that the inhabitants were
and it seemed comfort to
confusions of worldly affa
mind in general tho melar
ught of the dangers I wa
fear I was not prepared
in small hand on p
tray pencil commonplace

distemper I was seized with it

opening the house-door, she stoo
d, hesitating whether she ough

e set at great distance from this world,
t, it then appeared to me a vain, toilsom
bitants were strangely wandered, lost, &
comfort to me that I was so separatec
vorldly affairs, by my present affliction&
al tho melancholy was yet in a quiet frame
ngers I was in, it was not without a deep
prepared for Death, & I did set myself to

geld, &c., the alterations, which he produces, causes

belonged to no body, as ...

been him

ng the voices of a vast number of beings in

y mind and soon carried my ideas much intc

o be very much ravishd with it & sometimes

ıce. had scarce any definite ideas ... hear the sound. or rather t ... kn

felt like a wave in the air, held there by the

omething delirious & sometimes soft yet I w

gree Rational, and consulted with myself abı

s in my imagination only. I thought of speak

But

it dif

my c

oler

o h

lace

bewil

rom

dang

wher

con

see

o wrote an,
the Romans. T

the other hand

World, I used to be ve

felt soft, or in a sort

rdly knew who or what I was,

, and thereby the musick , a

ous and therefore lost m I was

consulted with myself about it &

and was ready

.ings

riding

.tself not so

. the light eith

. St. or i

itself not so

s the light eith

of leaves and

whether the new earth, but lately drawn a...

But if the world should ... heavenly ether retained still some elemen...

in, will fail you like a Broken Teeth or a foot ...

you like a Broken Tooth, or a foot out of joint.

intercepting … the pages

[illegible] and covering the pages

pursuing shadows & things ,

shadows & things, that I know are

on en ed, tos. eir d, bje ays ni. tec wa nse arch e na rib. o en r the bonc uty

effect silk codes would have on
agents in the field, he answered that
or what shall I say to you
ıfort to me that I was so separate
tage—our lives are all exceeding brittle
could hide behind the silk
In common
eluctance—Remember Lot's wife

ʼ̃ ̃

ʻe a han|
This s|ʯo
ill follo|
the mo|ʯ ʃ
Whom|ʯ ʃ
en dea|
etched|
this by
s not
death|
tom|*Still*
your
de ty
you
as a

something delirious and therefore lost I was to a degree rational ,
and consulted with myself about it & concluded it was in my

ook
ne sk
mong
ets of
leam
nat the
verythir
aw there
hildren.

tosses me 73 nd fro

1379 151 1379 1713-17 and fro

d indeed a sweetness and
to loose, but as I grew well I
atural to concern mvself with
eclared intention to seek a love union with an immortal
out to be Cynthia, a symbol of light and the
and into ultimate real
n scalatic stage rst objects sic's co th.
st the chief happiness and perfecti

What shall I leave to you or what shall I say to you
as it were wait for the judgment of (
rentions and connexions of the imaginations.
! rivers, by the laws of most nations, and by the natural p
s, is attributed to the proprietors of their banks, except-
as the Rhine or the Danube, which seem too large to fol- t it
ı to the property of the neighbouring fields. Yet even the
ısidered as the property of that nation, through whose contribute
something while I live that may bulk to corres- ne
bear them such a relation in the fancy.
which are made to land, bordering upon rivers, follow xt
'ilians, provided it be made by what they call *alluvion*,
ıd imperceptibly; which are circumstances, that assist y
e conjunction.
ıy considerable portion torn at once from one bank and err
becomes not *his* property, whose land it falls on, till it or
nd till the trees and plants have spread their roots into
e thought does not suffice exceedingly brittle and uncertain.....
ever distinguish between the necessity of a separation
n's possession, and the rules, which assign particular
persons. The first necessity is obvious, strong, and in-

th commentary/nd

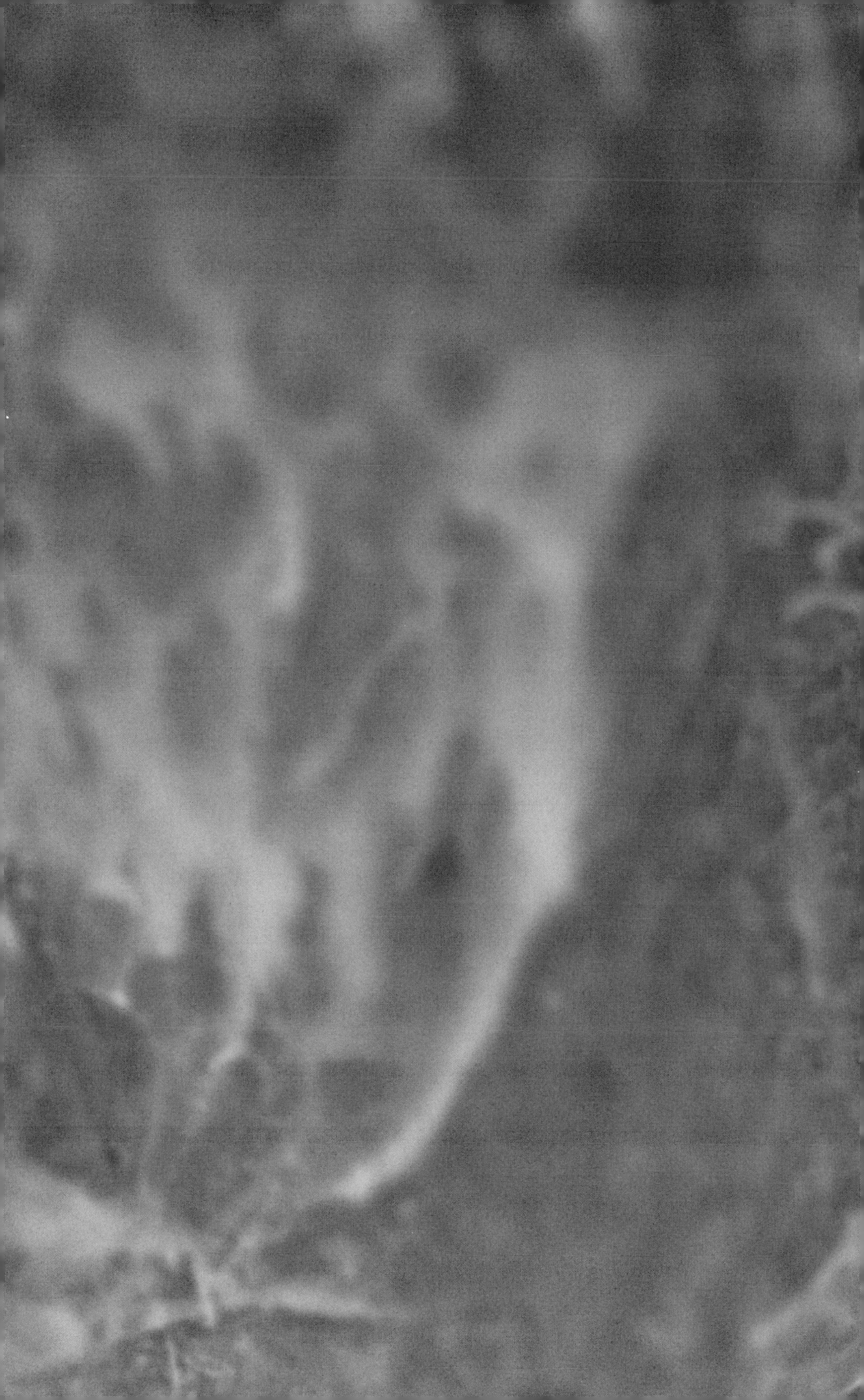

I remember the summer before my sister Jerusha's death,

making

and I was leaning over the south fence and thinking in this manner, that I was never likely to do better and where should I go etc.

...arked by the distortion of her... among the m

....& when I

lost, or at a Rive

direct me home.

fail— a field of r

....& when

lost, or at a Riv

direct me hom

fail— a field of

sed to ha
itself not so
s sp nto
s the light eith
is touc
its judge's face; bu
Not yet had the pir

nly heard as what might h
hat the mystery of the wo
riginal wild unbounded place
somewhat broken counterpoir
now we can rest in the empt
e absolute can ever be looked
e here actual-infinite of any sort
y haunts our being loosened fr
vocalism and remembering of

the
as yet
g moon ren
yh hang poised ft,
riftnt air, nor had
rl at he far reaches
oth land and
ew at d, or swim e
nild , flu of things o
odds for

and as new made unknown story

oy the moral alibi, 'Others, not I, are looking'.
akes use of others as a mirror in order to look at
:onscience !

teller . The country people, the sylvan dei

Glorious—what do we
surprisingly Beautiful—and
made manifest and the
over the surface would ec
erase the letters ·

frc .olden was tha
Na npel, without a
ıd did the right. T
o threatening words
.ablets ; no suppliant
its judge's face ; bu
Not yet had the pir
; ther
was no need at a ng br
, secure from war's alarms, p ll of

er that my spirits were (as the c

…e sound, or rather to have strong a

on of before. My ideas were of its bei

e other world. I used to be very muc

what I was but felt like a wave i

ınd remaining so insensible a

, without one chain of thoug

ıg and covering the pages. Th

ravished with it, and someti

her hands and the

n the air, held there by the m

the a like how so lik ering stoc

rn. This held a day or two, and then began to cr

Mirth is like a flash of lightning through

a cloud, and glitters for a moment.

Wi. o wintry cold, that the mother v
ressec v-pane with her thimbled f-
olden in; when th
A

always in sight of happiness & never get to it but just within

of motion,

there is no dead and complete silen
is "sitting careless" on a "granary
oft-lifted" in light movement "by tl
image also suggesting that the chaf
ie same direction in the wind, resemb

an
addled instance
gust of the harvester "o
tly rises and falls i
aid aside in stillnes
ops "twined flowers."
y on stepping stones
rhaps to a complete

To behold the oppressions that are done under the sun

:ave
iind.
form
om fle
ning-w
g on t
d lang
are the
esh lay

lead in the

in chase of happiness if you lean upon an arm of flesh
you must at las

abiding place but ought not a confederation
anged in fair Order, at her sig
nd sing her welcome She along th me
who come weary and heavy laden
What a bleak account I have drawn up against
I look forward Oh my soul
lutes them all with Honours du

all the organs consisting of little threads, or nerves: by the way
as frequently happiness
some parenthesis which darkens the sense

Haughtiness is always little violence

fluminaque obliquis cinxit declivia ripis,

in cruse of happiness if you lean upon an arm of flesh

you in death, and men

shall have power to part not

mine and his, be ye er

only hope is from this world

is not for the clay to say to the potter why have you made

be laid togethe

differing in having

s the poor body of one, and

the marks of

sudden

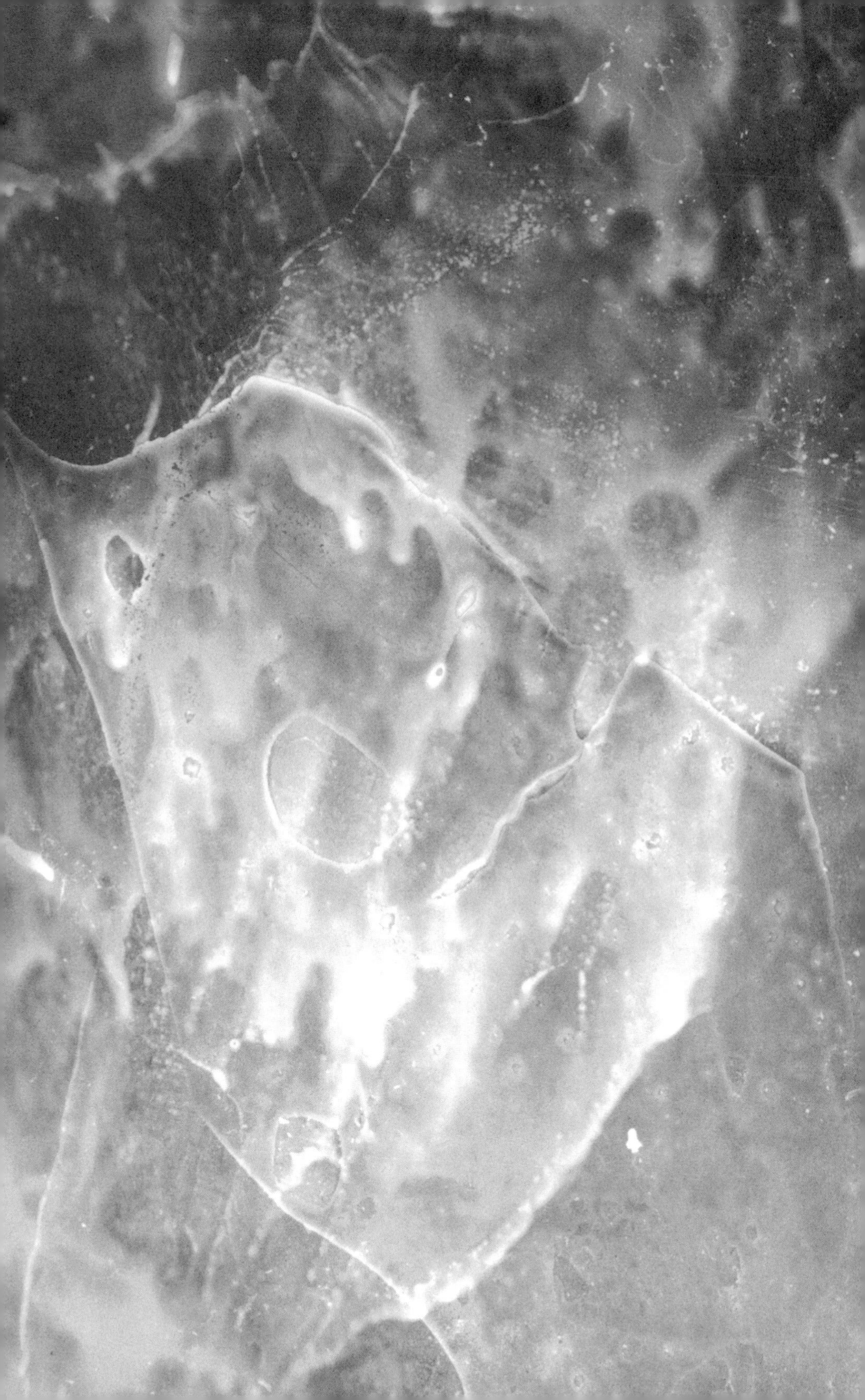

THAT THIS

Day is a type when visible

objects change then put

on form but the anti-type

That thing not shadowed

Type = 1st figure
ant-type = later "
→ She's challenging / inverting
typological rdg

The way music is formed of
cloud and fire once actually

concrete now accidental as
half truth or as whole truth

Is light anything like this

stray pencil commonplace

copy as to one aberrant

onward-gliding mystery

A secular arietta variation
Grass angels perish in this

harmonic collision because
non-being cannot be ‘this’

Not spirit not space finite

Not infinite to those fixed—

That this millstone as such

Quiet which side on which—

Is one mind put into another
in us unknown to ourselves
by going about among trees
and fields in moonlight or in
a garden to ease distance to
fetch home spiritual things

That a solitary person bears

witness to law in the ark to

an altar of snow and every

age or century for a day *is*

The pg. is a turn
→strophe
+
→anti-strophe

:en him carrying home in his handkerchief
ent stones and moss and flowers, which he
ıded to paint from nature exactly as they were.
ancient Rome and some
. I ask a or on the banks of the Tiber, making
:hed th s of everything that struck his fancy. I have
inguished rank among the greatest painters of
v. He replied, simply: "Je n'ai rien négligé."